YOUR KNOWLEDGE HAS VALUE

Bibliographic information published by the German National Library:

The German National Library lists this publication in the National Bibliography; detailed bibliographic data are available on the Internet at http://dnb.dnb.de .

Imprint:

Copyright © 2016 GRIN Verlag, Open Publishing GmbH
Print and binding: Books on Demand GmbH, Norderstedt Germany
ISBN: 9783668353411

This book at GRIN:

http://www.grin.com/en/e-book/345082/a-visual-analysis-of-jean-leon-gerome-s-the-muezzin-s-call-to-prayer

Michael Gorman

A Visual Analysis of Jean-Léon Gérôme's "The Muezzin's Call to Prayer"

GRIN Publishing

GRIN - Your knowledge has value

Since its foundation in 1998, GRIN has specialized in publishing academic texts by students, college teachers and other academics as e-book and printed book. The website www.grin.com is an ideal platform for presenting term papers, final papers, scientific essays, dissertations and specialist books.

A Visual Analysis of Jean-Léon Gérôme's *The Muezzin's Call to Prayer*

Michael Gorman
Salt Lake City
Original: 5 November, 2010
Modified November 2016

Content

1

Introduction

The purpose of this essay is to provide a visual analysis of Jean-Léon Gérôme's 1879 oil-painting: *A Muezzin Calling From The Top Of A Minaret The Faithful To Prayer* sometimes referred to simply as *The Muezzin's Call to Prayer*. For the sake of time and space, this essay will be using the latter title. This painting should not be confused with his similarly named (as well as thematically and visually similar) 1866 oil-painting: *The Muezzin (The Call to Prayer)*.

As stated previously, the painted was conceived in 1879 with oil on canvas. It is an example of Orientalism (part of the Realism movement) and is currently located in a private collection. Little information about where the painting was created can be ascertained—he was, however, known to have made many trips to Egypt during his lifetime, so it was likely that it was on one of these such trips that he created the painting. Is said to be about 25.98 inches wide x 35.83 inches tall.[1]

Before diving into the visual analysis, it may be appropriate to provide a brief biography of the artist and background for Orientalism. These sections of the essay will attempt brevity while providing as much background information as possible, so that the reader better understands the artist, movement, and the period and forces behind the painting. It will also be beneficial to provide some background on artistic principles and artistic elements.

---

[1] "Jean-Léon Gérôme, the Complete Works." *JeanleonGérôme.org*. 2016. Retrieved 2 November, 2016. http://www.jeanleonGérôme.org/A-Muezzin-Calling-From-The-Top-Of-A-Minaret-The-Faithful-To-Prayer.html.

Gérôme, Jean-Leon. *The Muezzin's Call to Prayer*. 1879. Private Collection. Unknown.

The Muezzin's Call to Prayer

Jean-Léon Gérôme

Jean-Léon Gérôme was a pioneering Orientalist painter and sculptor from Haute-Saône's Vesoul Prefecture (in France's Bourgogne-Franche-Comté region). He was born in 1824.[2] At about the age of 16, Gérôme went to Paris to study under Paul Delaroche. He later followed Delaroche to Italy between 1843 and 1844, where he visited such art capitals as Florence, Rome and the Vatican, and the ancient city of Pompeii.[3] It is possible that he intended to stay in Italy longer, but he cut his trip short in 1844 after falling ill. Following his return to France, Gérôme studied with Charles Gleyre before attending the École des Beaux-Arts.[4]

At this point in his life, his goal was to win the Prix de Rome, which he entered in 1846. He, however, failed to pass the final round because his "figure drawings were inadequate."[5] Despite this setback, one of his paintings (*The Cock Fight*) set in the Bay of Naples gained notable success with a third place prize at the Salon of 1847.[6] This piece became a symbolic representation of the "New-Grec" movement promoted by Charles Gleyre. With its sudden success, he forgot about his failures in the Prix de Rome and focused on other pieces for the Salons of 1848 and '49.[7]

These new successes soon brought his artistic talents into the interest of Napoleon III— which launched his career further still. With commissions from the emperor and his court, in 1852, Gérôme was able to fund his first trips to the Near-East.

---

[2] Ackerman, Gerald. *La Vie et l'œuvre de Jean-Léon Gérôme* , Paris, France: ACR Édition, 2000.

[3] Ackerman, Gerald. *La Vie et l'œuvre de Jean-Léon Gérôme* , Paris, France: ACR Édition, 2000.

[4] Ackerman, Gerald. *La Vie et l'œuvre de Jean-Léon Gérôme* , Paris, France: ACR Édition, 2000.

[5] "Jean-Léon Gérôme, the Complete Works." *JeanleonGérôme.org*. 2016. Retrieved 2 November, 2016. http://www.jeanleonGérôme.org/biography.html.

[6] "Musée d'Orsay, the Neo-Grec Period." *musee-orsay.fr*. 2006. Retrieved 2 November, 2016. http://www.musee-orsay.fr/en/events/exhibitions/in-the-musee-dorsay/exhibitions-in-the-musee-dorsay-more/page/1/article/jean-leon-Gérôme-25691.html?cHash=21536b366b.

[7] Ackerman, Gerald. *La Vie et l'œuvre de Jean-Léon Gérôme* , Paris, France: ACR Édition, 2000.

His first artistic travels brought him to Istanbul, Anatolia, and Greece. He was soon receiving commissions for various nobles, socialites, and cathedrals all over Paris. In 1856, Gérôme first visited Egypt.[8,9,10]

With his first trip to Egypt, Gérôme's career took a turn from Neo-Grec to Orientalism (both of which fall under the Academicism realm of Realism). Many of his paintings would depict Arab religion and North African landscapes. With this change in his subject matter, his success as an artist grew considerably. In 1858 he was commissioned to help decorate the Parisian home of Napoleon I's nephew (and Napoleon III's cousin). He later attempted a return to the Neo-Grec movement, but discovered that his work in this area found little interest with patrons or the public— thus forcing his hand back toward Orientalism.[11]

By the 1860s, Gérôme got married to the daughter of an art dealer, started his own school of art, and became a member of the Institut de France (a famous academic society). He continued to receive honors and awards throughout the decade, not only in France us also in Britain and Prussia. He was even invited to the grand opening of the Suez Canal in 1869, and became a professor at the École des Beaux-Arts.[12,13]

At this point, Expressionism and Impressionism were budding movements in Europe. In a return to the Salon in the 1870s, Gérôme initially protested these movements— not caring for their "decadence" and the artistic interpretation that

[8] "Musée d'Orsay, Gérôme's Imanginary Orients." *musee-orsay.fr*. 2006. Retrieved 2 November, 2016. http://www.musee-orsay.fr/en/events/exhibitions/in-the-musee-dorsay/exhibitions-in-the-musee-dorsay-more/page/5/article/jean-leon-Gérôme-25691.html?cHash=93a48a4db2.

[9] Ackerman, Gerald. *La Vie et l'œuvre de Jean-Léon Gérôme* , Paris, France: ACR Édition, 2000.

[10] Rosenthal, Donald A. *Orientalism, the Near East in French painting, 1800-1880*. Rochester, New York: Memorial Art Gallery of the University of Rochester, 1982.

[11] Ackerman, Gerald. *La Vie et l'œuvre de Jean-Léon Gérôme* , Paris, France: ACR Édition, 2000.

[12] Ackerman, Gerald. *La Vie et l'œuvre de Jean-Léon Gérôme* , Paris, France: ACR Édition, 2000.

[13] Weinberg, H. Barbara. *Thomas Eakins, Philadelphia Museum of Art*, metmuseum.org. October 2004. Retrieved 2 November 2016. http://www.metmuseum.org/toah/hd/eapa/hd_eapa.htm

accompanied them. [14] This dislike stemmed from his own Academic and Realist background which promotes and appreciates the artistic ability to copy onto canvas what the artists' eyes see in fine detail. They were two greatly contrasting and opposing schools are art. Unfortunately, Gérôme's public outcry against Impressionism initially setback his influence and career. His career and face in the public eye did recover in the 1880s after declaring that the style was "not so bad as I thought" after reportedly viewing some of Édouard Manet's work. [15]

The last years of Gérôme's life saw him welcome the growing popularity of photography, for the photograph could do exactly which Academic and Realistic painters had been attempting to do for as long as humans have been painting— copying with accuracy the world around as it truly was. Gérôme is quoted as declaring: "Thanks to photography, Truth has at last left her well." [16]

Gérôme's career and life came to and end one January in 1904. He was given a small funeral, which was attended by a former President of the French Republic, as well as many other politicians and famous artists and writers. He was buried in Paris, across from a statue that he had sculpted himself. [17]

[14] Seed, John. "Jon Swihart: Jean-Léon Gérôme Is His Master." *The Huffington Post.* 12 August, 201. Retrieved 3 November, 2016. http://www.huffingtonpost.com/john-seed/jon-swihart-jean-leon-ger_b_678758.html.

[15] Seed, John. "Jon Swihart: Jean-Léon Gérôme Is His Master." *The Huffington Post.* 12 August, 201. Retrieved 3 November, 2016. http://www.huffingtonpost.com/john-seed/jon-swihart-jean-leon-ger_b_678758.html.

[16] "Jean-Léon Gérôme, the Complete Works." *JeanleonGérôme.org.* 2016. Retrieved 2 November, 2016. http://www.jeanleonGérôme.org/biography.html.

[17] Ackerman, Gerald. *La Vie et l'œuvre de Jean-Léon Gérôme* , Paris, France: ACR Édition, 2000.

Orientalism

The Orientalism art movement (as previously mentioned) falls within the Academicism realm of Realism. Academicism, as one might imagine, is the "adherence to formal or conventional rules and traditions in art or literature."[18] This essentially contrasted with anything the expressionism and impressionism represented as budding movements. Realism in art is the attempt to represent a subject realistically and accurately, without including the addition of the incredible or imaginary— it is the "representation of people or things as they actually are."[19] Although many Orientalists sensationalized their subject matter and can be said to have used Impressionism in their subjects (including Gérôme) the style of art was still intended to be photographic. One can see why Gérôme would be so initially opposed to the work of Manet and others like him.

Orientalism is a style of art that adheres to the rules and conventions set by Realism, to realistically portray on canvas what the artist sees in oriental settings. The setting and theme of Orientalism can span from Egypt and North Africa, to Persia and the Near East, to China and Japan in the Far East. One might even make an argument for Greek settings in the genre. Orientalism is not just confined to the world of fine art, but it crosses the borders into of literary studies, history, architecture, philosophy and theology, geography, and anthropology.[20] This genre largely came about in Europe in the 19th, when European powers began vying for control of Asian resources and territory.

In the fine arts Western Asia and North Africa were the primary subjects portrayed, as these areas were more easily accessible from Europe. Eventually the

---

[18] Concise Oxford English Dictionary: Luxury Edition, s.v. "Academicism," Stevenson, Angus and Maurice Waite.

[19] Concise Oxford English Dictionary: Luxury Edition, s.v. "Realism," Stevenson, Angus and Maurice Waite.

[20] Sardar, Ziauddin. *Orientalism*. United Kingdom: McGraw-Hill Education, 1999.

artists became known simply as Orientalists in France (where the genre took off stronger than in other areas due to France's colonization of North Africa). Jean-Leon Gérôme became the honorary president of the Société des Peintres Orientalistes Français (founded in 1893).[21]

Before the 19th century, artistic portrayals of Moors and Ottoman Turks were common subjects in Medieval and Renaissance art. Biblical figures were also often portrayed in Middle-Eastern garb. These types of paintings can be thought of as "pre-orientalism." The early interest in Middle-Eastern and North African art came from Eastern Europe and Venice's conflict with the Ottoman Empire, the crusades, Spain's struggle against the Moors, and biblical images. Depictions and interest in the "exotic" has always interested Western cultures, Europeans often traveled and vacationed in these regions to get a taste of the exotic and have portraits of themselves made in local garb (this was evidently done by many who had never even left Europe).[22] One such European was Lord Byron, who sparked an interest in Europeans with his poetry other works of Romanticism. As mentioned previously, this took hold most notably in France.[23]

When Napoleon I entered Egypt in 1798 (still a servant of the Republic), we made archeological and cultural studies of the country— which further stimulated France's interest (despite Napoleon I's military failures in the theater).[24,25] Napoleon I's campaign in Egypt would become some of the earliest and most recognizable images in Orientalist art. Some of these notable pieces include: Antoine-Jean Gros's *Bonaparte*

---

[21] Bloom, Jonathan M. and Sheila Blair. *The Grove Encyclopedia of Islamic Art and Architecture: Volume 2*. Oxford, United Kingdom: Oxford University Press, 2009.

[22] Riding, Christine. "Travellers and Sitters: The Orientalist Portrait." *The Lure of the East: British Orientalist Painting*, ed. Tromans. London: Tate Publishing, 2008. Pages 48-61.

[23] Cochran, Peter. *Byron and Orientalism*. Newcastle, United Kingdom: Cambridge Scholars Press. 2006.

[24] Harding, James, *Artistes Pompiers: French Academic Art in the 19th Century*, United Kingdom: Academy Editions, 1979.

[25] *Description de l'Égypte*. Paris, France: Le Gouvernement Francias, 1809-1822.

Visiting the Plague Victims of Jaffa in1804, *the Battle of Abukir* in 1806, and *Napoleon at the Battle of the Pyramids* in 1810, as well as Anne-Louis Girodet de Roussy-Trioson's *La Révolte du Caire* of 1810. From this point the Orientalist movement became a style in its own right, helping bring the "exotic" to Europe. Contemporary events in the region also became of interest, such as the Barbary Wars, the Greek war for independence from the Ottoman Empire, the colonization of Africa, etc.

Much of these early works (before Realism took over the genre) often portrayed the "Orient" as exotic, fanciful, sensual, romantic, and stereotyped. Islam, Harems, and Turkish baths were common subjects within Orientalism. Although Gérôme was more inclined toward realism, he was not exempt from Romantic movements or the sensualization of his art. These sorts of depictions are (as reportedly said by Nicholas Tromans) responsible for "the equation of Orientalism with the nude in pornographic mode,"[26] meaning that a sort of fetish has grown towards the "Orient" as a result of sensualized Orientalist art.[27]

At any rate, with the growth of photography, and modern art Orientalism as a painted art form died down. Most westerners seeking the "exotic" could take their own photographs or view the photographs of others. Realism persisted and promulgated with accurate portrayals of the Near East, but the Romance and search for the exotic never quite passed with the art form. So concludes the segments on Orientalism and the life and work of Jean-Léon Gérôme— the artist who was born into a French society that was just coming into the Orientalist movement, helped promulgate the genre and bring it to its height, then passed away with the genre with the birth of popular photography.

---

[26] Tromans, Nicholas. *The Lure of the East, British Orientalist Painting*, United Kingdom: Tate Publishing, 2008.

[27] "Musée d'Orsay, Gérôme's Imanginary Orients." *musee-orsay.fr*. 2006. Retrieved 2 November, 2016. http://www.musee-orsay.fr/en/events/exhibitions/in-the-musee-dorsay/exhibitions-in-the-musee-dorsay-more/page/5/article/jean-leon-Gérôme-25691.html?cHash=93a48a4db2.

Artistic Principles and Elements

In terms of art visualization, the process can be broken down into two categories: the artistic principles and artistic elements. These aspects of images are what make a piece of art visually appealing. One might have the most beautiful image or subject matter in the world, but if they cannot coordinate the various elements and principles, the image becomes void of artistic value.

The artistic principles consist of balance, proportion, emphasis, variety, movement, rhythm, and harmony. Balance is the visual weight and size of objects in an image and how they play off of one another and spread out information across a plane. In terms of balance, there are three types that can be expressed: symmetrical, asymmetrical, and radial. Symmetrical balance is when the objects in an image of similar size and scale mirror one another on the plane so that the image is balanced on two sides. Asymmetrical balance is when objects of different proportions fill out a plane but still create equal weight on two halves. Radial balance occurs when the distribution of images is centered around a focal point in all directions as opposed to splitting the image in half.[28]

Proportion takes into account the scale of objects in an image and their ratio to one another. This principle is important so that the scale of the image and objects in a piece of art make visual sense and. For example, if there is an image of a person standing next to a tree, then the size of the tree should be in proportion to the size of the person (meaning that the tree should be larger than the person to a certain degree and that if the tree is smaller then it can imply that the person is a giant (if placement does not also indicate that the tree is in the background).[29]

---

[28] "Principles of Art." *learn..* learn.leighcotnoir.com. 2016. Retrieved 3 November, 2016. http://learn.leighcotnoir.com/artspeak/principles/.

[29] "Principles of Art." *learn..* learn.leighcotnoir.com. 2016. Retrieved 3 November, 2016. http://learn.leighcotnoir.com/artspeak/principles/.

Emphasis comes into play when one object or element of an image stands out more than the another. This is used to give that object a sense of importance and attention. It can also be used to convey a message or certain sentiments. An example might be a red flower in a field of lavender. [30]

Variety creates interest in an image and reduces monotony by changing an object or mixing different elements. It can create diversity by using contrasting images or several distinct patterns as opposed to one or two. In a crowd of people, it would not be particularly interesting to have a group of faceless men all wearing black and having the same hat, to eliminate this visually unappealing mess some of the individuals should be women and children, they should very in height, they might wear different hats or none at all, more color might be introduced, etc.[31]

Movement is the visual flow of an image, the path that the viewers' eyes follow across the image from one object to another. One might think that their gaze is random or unintended, but by using focal points and other principles the artist can create a path for movement. It is used to decided what the viewer will view first, then where their eyes will go next.[32]

Rhythm is the most difficult of the principles to explain or conceptualize, but it has been described as "a continuance, a flow, or a feeling of movement achieved by the repetition of regulated visual information."[33] So in a way it is closely linked to the movement principle and might even be considered part of its directive.

---

[30] "Elements & Principles of Art." *project ARTiculate*. projectarticulate.org. 2006. Retrieved 3 November, 2016. http://www.projectarticulate.org/principles.php.

[31] "Principles of Art." *learn.*. learn.leighcotnoir.com. 2016. Retrieved 3 November, 2016. http://learn.leighcotnoir.com/artspeak/principles/.

[32] "Principles of Art." *learn.*. learn.leighcotnoir.com. 2016. Retrieved 3 November, 2016. http://learn.leighcotnoir.com/artspeak/principles/.

[33] "Principles of Art." *learn.*. learn.leighcotnoir.com. 2016. Retrieved 3 November, 2016. http://learn.leighcotnoir.com/artspeak/principles/.

The final artistic principle is harmony. Harmony in art is when an image has a visually satisfying appeal created from the objects in an image (as conceived by the other principles and elements). This is most often done by combining and pairing related objects with similar shapes, sizes, colors, etc.[34]

There are seven artistic elements are line, color, shape, form, value, space, and texture. Like the artistic principles, the elements are used to transform a simple image into a visually appealing work of art. The artistic elements are more used to distinguish the objects in an image rather than their placement, but spacing is a part of that as well.

The first and simplest element to explain is Line. The lines of an image (as with all lines) are the movement of a point through space. Lines in an image can be used to distinguish or bold an image. The use of lines can play a heavy role in the genre and style of art used in an image. They can also be implied or hidden to create a more realistic image, while bolder lines can create a more "cartoony" or interpretive image.[35]

Color might logically come as the next element, coming from three primary colors (red, blue, and yellow) as well as black and white. They can vary in hue, value, and intensity to create any assortment and combination of pigment necessary for an artist to convey an emotion. Warm colors such as red and orange can often be comforting (as well as angry), while cooler colors such as blue express emotions such as depression, gloom, and sullenness.[36]

Next are shape and form. Related but distinct, it can be said that Shape is perceived in the 2nd dimension with spacing, while Form is perceived in the 3rd with

[34] "Principles of Art." *learn.*. learn.leighcotnoir.com. 2016. Retrieved 3 November, 2016. http://learn.leighcotnoir.com/artspeak/principles/.

[35] "Elements & Principles of Art." *project ARTiculate*. projectarticulate.org. 2006. Retrieved 3 November, 2016. http://www.projectarticulate.org/principles.php.

[36] "Elements & Principles of Art." *project ARTiculate*. projectarticulate.org. 2006. Retrieved 3 November, 2016. http://www.projectarticulate.org/principles.php.

depth (in addition to height and width). These elements are used to give an image depth and perspective, without them a small tree next to a person (as provided as an earlier example) is just a small tree (or a giant person), while shape and form tell the viewers eyes that the person is in the foreground and the tree is in the background.[37]

Value involves light and dark to create the perception of shadow and light. They can vary in their intensity and also play an important role in creating a 3rd dimensional space on a plane. Working with the element of space (the "area in which art is organized"), shape, and form, an image truly pops off of the page and comes to life.[38]

The final element, texture, is the visual or literal qualities perceived on surfaces of an image. Using shadows and colors (as well as other elements) an artist can create surfaces that appear smooth and flat, coarse, rugged, fabric-like, feather-like, etc. This creates a final detail that can make the viewer forget that they are staring at a plane instead of a scene outside of their window. Although texture is largely only visually representative and implied in an image, some artists go so far as to actually incorporate real 3rd dimensional surfaces in their art.[39]

Such are the various artistic principles and elements that one uses when creating and visually assessing an image or piece of art. There may be small differentials in the lists of these two artistic aspects, but for the most part they are universally accepted. With that, it is finally time to begin the visual analysis of *The Muezzin's Call to Prayer* (as shown at the beginning of the essay).

---

[37] "Elements & Principles of Art." *project ARTiculate.* projectarticulate.org. 2006. Retrieved 3 November, 2016. http://www.projectarticulate.org/principles.php.

[38] "Elements & Principles of Art." *project ARTiculate.* projectarticulate.org. 2006. Retrieved 3 November, 2016. http://www.projectarticulate.org/principles.php.

[39] "Elements & Principles of Art." *project ARTiculate.* projectarticulate.org. 2006. Retrieved 3 November, 2016. http://www.projectarticulate.org/principles.php.

Visual Analysis

Jean-Léon Gérôme's *The Muezzin's Call to Prayer* is an oil-on-canvas painting depicting a Muezzin (Islamic holy man) standing in a tower that is noticeably higher than any other tower or building in the city or surrounding area. The tower is being circled by birds, some of which are flying underneath it, indicating how high up the tower is. There is an onion-shaped dome at the top of the tower, which displays the Islamic symbol of a crescent moon. The man placed in the tower (in the top-left corner of the canvas above everything else) overlooks an urban setting in the lower right corner of the canvas. The city depicted has buildings with similar architecture to the tower that the Muezzin is standing in. The man is apparently calling out for the daily prayer (as suggested by the title).

Gérôme uses many of the principles and elements of art adequately to create a visually appealing image. As mentioned in the previous paragraph: the city in the lower part of the painting has many buildings similar to the tower that the Muezzin is standing in. The buildings have stereotypical Middle-Eastern architecture with onion-shaped dome-roofs. The use of this architecture plays into the principle of harmony nicely, giving the tower something to connect it with the rest of the city in the painting. The use of color also plays into Harmony. All of the buildings in the city are either white or a very pale shade of earth-colors, like beige and tan.

While the buildings depicted in the painting are all similar in architecture, they also have slight differences which when added up gives them variety. Some of the onion-shaped domes are more detailed that others. There is a dome that is being partially shown in the bottom-left corner, which is in front of the main tower (where the the Muezzin standing). The dome in the corner displays elaborate, vine-like designs carved into it, while the dome on top of the main tower has no designs on it and is paneled. The rest of the domes and towers throughout the city in the bottom of the painting are all depicted in various shapes and heights. Some of the domes are tall and

14

narrow while some have greater girth than height. Some of them are distinctly larger than others.

Proportion and movement work as one in this painting. The viewer's eyes are first drawn to the main tower and the muezzin standing in it, as it is the second closest thing to the viewer in the painting. The viewer's eyes are then brought to the birds circling above the tower. The viewers would then probably notice the fraction of an onion-shaped dome in the bottom-left corner of the page, which is slightly overlapping the main tower. The bird, flying underneath the main tower (to the right of the dome in the bottom-left corner) would probably be the next thing the viewer would notice. The bird below the main tower sets up the viewers gaze to follow the city as it fades out into the distance.

The principles of proportion and movement are aided by emphasis and balance. The emphasis of the painting is the main tower. More specifically the emphasis of the painting is the man in the tower. The man standing in the main tower is the Muezzin, calling out to prayer, making him the focus point of the painting (since the painting is called *The Muezzin's Call to Prayer*). The Muezzin's tower stands out so much because it is the closest (fully shown) object in the painting. It runs from the top of the canvas to the bottom and takes up nearly the entire left half of the canvas. The main tower is higher up than anything else in the painting, giving into the notion that since it is higher up then it is more important. The painting has asymmetrical balance since the Muezzin's tower takes up the left half of the canvas, and the city only takes up the bottom of the right half, leaving a clear pale-blue sky in the top-right of the canvas (also putting further emphasis in the main tower). Gérôme makes up for the lack of occupied space on the right side of the canvas by making the less occupied area much lighter than the side that has the Muezzin's tower.

The lines in the painting form a fairly balanced use of organic and geometric shapes. The majority of the buildings in the painting have geometric bases and bodies with round, onion-shaped dome-roofs. The Muezzin and the mountains in the

15

background are also composed of organic shapes. Since the painting is in an urban setting, there are many buildings overlapping each other (to help form perspective as the city draws back in the distance) creating many unusual lines where two shapes meet.

Gérôme uses a variety of texture throughout the painting. The onion-shaped dome in the bottom left corner of the page has elaborate, abstract designs carved into it. This gives it the appearance of a bumpy or lifted texture. The dome on top of the Muezzin's tower appears not to have designs but instead has a smooth paneled texture to it. It is difficult to comprehend the textures of the buildings as they fade further into the distance. For the most part, the remaining buildings appear to have course stone bodies, while the remaining onion-domes appear smooth and polished.

In the painting, Gérôme also uses the elements of space and value to correspond with perspective. The objects in the painting that are closer to the viewer are darker, as it would appear that they are begin hidden behind a mountain or another large object that is not depicted on the canvas. As the objects in the painting recede, color fades but their value brightens (up). This is also the case in the spacing of the items. Most of the buildings in the city are spaced relatively close together, leaving less room for shadows and more area for the light to hit. The buildings that are closer are spaced farther apart have more area to cast shadows in the painting.

Using these principles and elements, Jean-Léon Gérôme created a visually appealing Orientalist (European depictions of Asia and the Middle-Eastern world during European colonialism in the nineteenth century) style painting. All of the principles and elements he used work together and accent each other, giving them a far greater effect then they would have just by themselves. Color and Harmony, as well as the combination of Proportion, Movement, Emphasis, and Balance, were some of the combinations that Gérôme used to guide the viewers' eyes and make the Muezzin's tower stand out in the painting. He also combines, space, shape, and line to give the city a clustered feeling to balance out the painting.

16

Primary Sources

Description de l'Égypte. Paris, France: Le Gouvernement Francias, 1809-1822.

Secondary Sources

Ackerman, Gerald. *La Vie et l'œuvre de Jean-Léon Gérôme* , Paris, France: ACR Édition, 2000.

Bloom, Jonathan M. and Sheila Blair. *The Grove Encyclopedia of Islamic Art and Architecture: Volume 2*. Oxford, United Kingdom: Oxford University Press, 2009.

Cochran, Peter. *Byron and Orientalism*. Newcastle, United Kingdom: Cambridge Scholars Press. 2006.

Concise Oxford English Dictionary: Luxury Edition, s.v. "Academicism," Stevenson, Angus and Maurice Waite.

Concise Oxford English Dictionary: Luxury Edition, s.v. "Realism," Stevenson, Angus and Maurice Waite.

"Elements & Principles of Art." *project ARTiculate*. projectarticulate.org. 2006. Retrieved 3 November, 2016. http://www.projectarticulate.org/principles.php.

Harding, James, *Artistes Pompiers: French Academic Art in the 19th Century*, United Kingdom: Academy Editions, 1979.

17

"Jean-Léon Gérôme, the Complete Works." *JeanleonGérôme.org*. 2016. Retrieved 2 November, 2016. http://www.jeanleonGérôme.org/A-Muezzin-Calling-From-The-Top-Of-A-Minaret-The-Faithful-To-Prayer.html.

"Jean-Léon Gérôme, the Complete Works." *JeanleonGérôme.org*. 2016. Retrieved 2 November, 2016. http://www.jeanleonGérôme.org/biography.html.

"Musée d'Orsay, Gérôme's Imanginary Orients." *musee-orsay.fr*. 2006. Retrieved 2 November, 2016. http://www.musee-orsay.fr/en/events/exhibitions/in-the-musee-dorsay/exhibitions-in-the-musee-dorsay-more/page/5/article/jean-leon-Gérôme-25691.html?cHash=93a48a4db2.

"Musée d'Orsay, the Neo-Grec Period." *musee-orsay.fr*. 2006. Retrieved 2 November, 2016. http://www.musee-orsay.fr/en/events/exhibitions/in-the-musee-dorsay/exhibitions-in-the-musee-dorsay-more/page/1/article/jean-leon-Gérôme-25691.html?cHash=21536b366b.

"Principles of Art." *learn.*. learn.leighcotnoir.com. 2016. Retrieved 3 November, 2016. http://learn.leighcotnoir.com/artspeak/principles/.

Riding, Christine. "Travellers and Sitters: The Orientalist Portrait." *The Lure of the East: British Orientalist Painting*, ed. Tromans. London: Tate Publishing, 2008. Pages 48-61.

Rosenthal, Donald A. *Orientalism, the Near East in French painting, 1800-1880*. Rochester, New York: Memorial Art Gallery of the University of Rochester, 1982.

Sardar, Ziauddin. *Orientalism*. United Kingdom: McGraw-Hill Education, 1999.

Seed, John. "Jon Swihart: Jean-Léon Gérôme Is His Master." *The Huffington Post*. 12
August, 201. Retrieved 3 November, 2016.
http://www.huffingtonpost.com/john-seed/jon-swihart-jean-leon-
ger_b_678758.html.

Tromans, Nicholas. *The Lure of the East, British Orientalist Painting*, United Kingdom:
Tate Publishing, 2008.

Weinberg, H. Barbara. *Thomas Eakins, Philadelphia Museum of Art*, metmuseum.org.
October   2004.   Retrieved   2   November   2016.
http://www.metmuseum.org/toah/hd/eapa/hd_eapa.htm

Image Sources

Gérôme, Jean-Leon. *The Muezzin's Call to Prayer*. 1879. Private Collection.
Unknown.

YOUR KNOWLEDGE HAS VALUE